S0-AWT-495

Discarded From
Saint Andrew's School Library

INDIA
the culture

Bobbie Kalman

SAINT ANDREWS SCHOOL LIBRARY
13601 SARATOGA AVE
P. O. BOX 2789
SARATOGA, CA 95070

The Lands, Peoples, and Cultures Series

Toronto·Oxford·New York· Crabtree Publishing Company

The Lands, Peoples, and Cultures Series
Created by Bobbie Kalman

Written by
Bobbie Kalman
Margaret Hoogeveen
Christine Arthurs

Editor-in-Chief
Bobbie Kalman

Editors
Christine Arthurs
Margaret Hoogeveen
Janine Schaub

Design
Heather Delfino

Pasteup
Adriana Longo

Printer
Worzalla Publishing Company
Stevens Point, Wisconsin

Illustrations
Halina Below-Spada: Back cover
Karen Harrison: p. 17; Bernadette Lau: p.21.

Photography acknowledgments
Cover: Sudha and Abdullah Khandwani
Chris Beeman: p.16(bottom); Mary Bredin: p.23; Ian Clifford/E-Side Studios: p.24(bottom);
R.C. Doyle/Masterfile: p.20; Ken Faris: p.12; Jeremy Ferguson/First Light: p.5, 18-19, 31(bottom);
David Gledhill: p.11; Catriona Gordon: p.4, 10, 16(top); Ron Hayes: p.6, 18(left);
Courtesy of India Tourist Organization: p.13(bottom), 27; Mia and Klaus/Four by Five: p.14;
Sudha & Abdullah Khandwani: p.8, 13(top), 15(top and bottom), 24(top), 25, 26;
Larry Rossignol: p.7, 31(top); Royal Ontario Museum: Title page; Shiv Sud: p.22;
J. Lentin/Zardoya/Canapress: p.9.

The title page shows a Hindu celebration in which huge wooden carts are pushed through the streets. The motif that appears in the heading of every section is the outline of the famous Taj Mahal. The stylized peacock on the back cover shows the magnificence of India's national bird.

In loving memory of Edith Crabtree

Cataloguing in Publication Data

Kalman, Bobbie, 1947-
   India, the culture

(Lands, peoples, and cultures series)
Includes index.

ISBN 0-86505-212-3 (bound) ISBN 0-86505-292-1 (pbk.)
1. India - Social life and customs - Juvenile literature.
2. India - Civilization - 1947- Juvenile Literature.
I. Title. II. Series.

DS421.K34 1990   j954   LC93-27372

Published by
Crabtree Publishing Company

350 Fifth Ave., Suite 3308	360 York Rd., RR#4	73 Lime Walk
New York,	Niagara-On-The-Lake,	Headington, Oxford
NY 10118	Ontario L0S 1J0	OX3 7AD

Copyright © 1990 CRABTREE PUBLISHING COMPANY.
All rights reserved. No part of this publication may be
reproduced, stored in a retrieval system or be transmitted
in any form or by any means, electronic, mechanical,
photocopying, recording, or otherwise, without the prior
written permission of Crabtree Publishing Company.

Contents

The culture of India combines ancient customs and brand-new ways. The people of India flock to cinemas to see the latest Indian films, but they also attend local plays that are over a thousand years old. Although Indians like modern ways, they treasure their traditions, which are as rich and varied as the people who live there.

India is a nation of people with strong religious convictions, yet people of different faiths can live side by side because the Indian people are tolerant of one another. People of many races, languages, and beliefs live together peacefully. As a result, a fascinating mixture of different types of art, dance, music, cuisine, and crafts flourish in India. There is also a wide variety of festivals and colorful celebrations.

Although there are many diverse traditions, the culture of India is unified in many respects. Over the centuries the ways of different peoples have blended together to create a cultural heritage that is truly national and distinctly Indian!

(left) This woman looks around while she waits for a ceremony to begin. She is a member of the Ladakhi community, whose culture is quite different from that of the rest of India. Her people have become part of the colorful fabric that makes up India.

(opposite) Parades and processions are popular events everywhere in India. Always colorful, these spectacles draw huge crowds.

Rooted in religion

Religion has affected every part of Indian life: the festivals celebrated, the clothes worn, the food eaten, the buildings constructed, and the stories told. To learn about the culture of India, it is important to understand its main religions. Two major world religions, Hinduism and Buddhism, originated in this land. Today Hindus make up almost eighty-three percent of India's population. Just over eleven percent are Muslims. Smaller numbers of Christians, Sikhs, Buddhists, Parsis, and Jains also live in India.

Hinduism

Over six hundred million Indians are Hindus. Hinduism is an ancient religion that has roots in the early Indus Valley civilization of three thousand years ago. Hindus believe in a supreme spiritual force called Brahman. Brahman, which has no form, is thought of as the "High God." This force controls all life and exists as three great beings: Brahma the Creator, Vishnu the Preserver, and Shiva the Changer.

Two of these main gods, Vishnu and Shiva, are believed to descend to earth from time to time. Taking human form they become deities called avatars who have many adventures on earth. For instance, Vishnu once descended to earth as the avatar Krishna. Shown in pictures as the handsome blue god of love, Krishna is popular among villagers because they believe that he was raised by peasants. The elephant-headed god, Ganesh, who is the god of luck and riches, is one of the most popular avatars of Vishnu. Kali is a well-known female deity. She is a destructive goddess who is feared by all. There are hundreds of avatars in Hinduism. Each of these minor gods is worshipped by his or her admirers. Although Hindus believe in one High God that exists within each person, they worship many different deities in their daily lives.

(above) Hindu temples are fantastic works of art. The outer walls are carved and colorfully painted from top to bottom. The statue in the middle is the popular elephant god Ganesh.

The cycle of life

Hindus believe a person can have many lives. This cycle of birth, death, and rebirth is called reincarnation. A person's position in life is determined by his or her *karma*. *Karma* is either a reward or a punishment. If you are good in this life, your karma will be good, and you will be rewarded with a good life the next time you are reborn. If you are evil, you will be punished with a miserable life. Hindus hope to break the cycle of reincarnation by achieving freedom from rebirth. In order to attain this state of everlasting peace, Hindus follow the law of *dharma*, which says that individuals must perform all the duties required by their positions in life.

The two main principles of Hinduism, *karma* and *dharma*, have shaped the structure of traditional Indian society. The laws of *dharma* led to the formation of the caste system. People were divided into groups based on the occupation and the social class into which they were born. Their children and their children's children stayed in the same castes. Although the caste system is now illegal in India, it still rules the lives of most people.

Ancient scriptures

Hinduism is based on ancient scriptures known collectively as the *Vedas*. *Veda* means "book of knowledge." For two thousand years the stories that make up the *Vedas* were passed from generation to generation by word of mouth until they were finally written down.

Indian literature is filled with the legends of the gods. The most famous stories are told in two epics, or long poems. The *Mahabharata* is the longest poem in existence. The *Ramayana* is another great poem. The *Puranas*, a collection of legends, is extremely popular because it tells funny stories about Krishna's childhood. All these works have inspired sculpture, art, drama, and dance. Because they are central to many cultural activities, most Indians know the stories by heart.

As a teenager, the god Krishna lived among peasants and worked as a cowherd. He is always depicted as blue.

Daily rituals

Hindus worship by performing daily rituals and small acts of worship called *pujas*. *Pujas* help Hindus purify themselves. Most Hindus have favorite gods to whom they pray every day and for whom they reserve a special corner of their homes. Here candles are lit and placed in front of pictures or statues of the gods. People also visit temples where they light incense in front of religious paintings or hang flower necklaces around statues. Brahmin priests help people with their religious practices.

Wandering holy men

Some Hindus become so devoted to their faith that they give up all worldly possessions and become wandering holy men called *sadhus*. Constantly moving from place to place, they are given food by other Hindus. They fill their solitary lives with religious exercises and meditation. Occasionally each *sadhu* visits his personal *guru*, a teacher of Hinduism who guides others in their search for holiness.

Islam

The Muslim religion is called Islam. Muslims are followers of the prophet Muhammad, who was born in the Persian city of Mecca in the year 570 A.D. According to Islamic belief, Muhammad was inspired by God, whom Muslims know as Allah. He wrote down Allah's messages of guidance in a sacred book called the *Koran*. With about eighty-eight million Muslims, India has one of the largest Islamic populations in the world. The religion of Islam was established in India after Muslim invaders took power in the thirteenth century.

The five duties

All Muslims are required to carry out five duties. They must believe that Allah is the only God and must pray five times a day. Muslims worship at mosques every Friday. When Muslims pray, they face in the direction of the holy city of Mecca and go through a series of bowing movements on their knees. They are required to give to the poor and carry out the month-long fast of *Ramadan* every year. During this time, Muslims do not eat or drink between sunrise and sunset. The fifth Muslim duty is to make at least one pilgrimage to Mecca.

Sikhism

In the early sixteenth century Guru Nanak, a wandering holy man, founded the Sikh religion. He taught his followers not to worship many deities as Hindus do, but to worship one God. Sikhs believe that by following their religion

faithfully they can be with God and avoid the cycle of reincarnation. Sikhs reject the Hindu caste system. They believe that all people should live and worship together as equals.

The Golden Temple of Amritsar

The beautiful Golden Temple in the city of Amritsar is the holy center of the Sikh religion. The Golden Temple has four main doors to welcome people coming from any direction. Sikhs make pilgrimages to the Golden Temple to learn from the *Granth Sahib*, the "Teacher Book," and to cleanse themselves in the holy waters surrounding the temple. Today over thirteen million Sikhs live in India, mostly in the state of Punjab.

A Sikh man wears five outward signs of his faith. All of these begin with the letter "k." He has long hair, or *kesh*, tied up in a bun and covered with a turban. He wears short pants called *kachha* and carries a comb called *kangha* and a small sword known as *kirpan*. His bracelet, called *kara*, symbolizes the idea that God is without beginning or end. After being baptized, men take the last name Singh, which means "lion," and women use the last name Kaur, which means "princess."

Buddhism

The founder of Buddhism, Siddhartha Gautama, lived in India in the fifth century B.C. For many years he traveled the country, thinking about the suffering of humanity. One day he meditated for a very long time and believed that he discovered a way to end suffering. He became the Buddha, or "Awakened One" and began preaching in Sarnath, near Varanasi, and then all over India.

Like Hindus, Buddhists believe in reincarnation. Central to Buddhism is meditation. This method of relaxing frees the mind of thought. The goal of Buddhist meditation is to feel peaceful—free of hatred, sadness, and desire.

Muslims worship five times a day. While praying, they face the holy city of Mecca, which is in Saudi Arabia.

Christianity

Most of India's fifteen million Christians live in the state of Kerala. Christians worship Jesus Christ whom they call the son of God. Thomas, one of the apostles of Jesus, is said to have traveled to southern India in the year 52 A.D., where he established a small Christian community. Christianity became more popular when European missionaries arrived in later years. Indian Christians have blended together traditional Indian and Christian customs. Christmas, for example, is celebrated just as many Hindu festivals are: with colorful parades, family gatherings, candles, and offerings of food.

Jainism

Mahavira was the founder of the Jain religion. He lived in the fifth century B.C., around the same time as the Buddha. Mahavira taught his followers to concentrate on good behavior, prayer, and meditation. His most important lesson was that people should never injure any living being. As a result, all Jains are vegetarians, and many do not eat root vegetables or anything that is red, the color of blood. The most devout Jains wear masks over their mouths and noses to make sure they do not breathe in and kill small insects. The Jain principle of non-violence has played a major role in shaping the character of the Indian people.

Living in harmony

Because religious feelings are so strong, and people of so many faiths live as neighbors in India, Indians place a high value on tolerance. Tolerance is a willingness to be patient towards people whose opinions and actions differ from one's own. India is an example of religious tolerance at work. People of many different faiths live together in harmony.

(above) The Sikhs' holy center is the Golden Temple of Amritsar in the state of Punjab. People travel to this shrine from all over India and the world.

Holy water

In order to survive, people need water. They depend on it for drinking, washing, and watering their crops and farm animals. Yet water means a great deal more to the majority of Indians. They believe water has sacred properties. Therefore, it is the focus of many of their religious rituals.

Mother Ganges

To purify themselves, Hindus often bathe in sacred rivers. According to Hindus, the holiest river of all is *Ganga Ma*, meaning "Mother Ganges." The Ganges River begins in the Himalayan Mountains, which is said to be the land of the gods. It flows 2506 kilometers (1,557 miles) before it empties into the Bay of Bengal. Hindus believe that the Ganges once flowed through the heavens, where it acquired strong purifying powers. Dedicated believers make pilgrimages to sacred spots along the Ganges River. Local people often provide pilgrims with food and shelter.

Some worshippers toss offerings of flowers, grain, or coins into the flowing river. Others make small boats out of leaves, fill them with petals, light small candles inside, and set them afloat. Sometimes pilgrims take jars filled with holy river water home with them. Many people travel to the riverside when they are close to death. To die while bathing in the Ganges River is the final wish of every devout Hindu. Others go to the sacred river to cremate their dead relatives along the banks and scatter their ashes into the water. Hindus believe that this ritual frees the deceased from the cycle of reincarnation.

(above) The stone steps that line the banks of the Ganges have been worn down by generations of worshippers.

City of light

Each year hundreds of thousands of pilgrims travel to Varanasi, the holiest city along the Ganges River. At one time Varanasi was called Kashi, which means "City of Light." Today all kinds of people, rich and poor, young and old, come to Varanasi from every corner of India. Pilgrims flock to the steps, or *ghats*, that lead down to the river. Here people wash themselves and their clothes. Others pray in the cross-legged lotus position. Priests and holy men perform rituals, read the scriptures, and offer advice. Pilgrims also visit some of the city's many temples, each one built in honor of a certain god. A complete tour of the temples, shrines, and special spots along the river takes about five days. Those who cannot make the trip to Varanasi themselves can still receive a blessing by touching a pilgrim who has just returned from there.

Khumb Mela

The largest celebration along the holy river occurs at Allahabad, where the Ganges joins the Yamuna River. According to Hindu legend a few drops of holy nectar once fell on this spot. To remember this event, a festival called the *Khumb Mela* is celebrated when the stars are aligned in a certain way. This occurs only once every twelve years. Nearly thirty million worshippers attended the last *Khumb Mela* in 1989. Pilgrims traveled to Allahabad aboard four hundred trains, five thousand boats, and six thousand buses. The *ghats* and surrounding religious sites overflowed with people praying and cleansing themselves in the holy water of the Ganges.

(above) As well as offerings of flowers and money, people throw everything into the Ganges River—including pop bottles, newspapers, and plastic bags.

Indian art

Indian artists have explored every possible art form. Elaborate temples and palaces, lifelike sculptures, bejeweled carvings, and golden paintings are just a few examples. Today India's artists are developing modern styles that draw on the rich traditions of their past. They are proud of their heritage.

Faith as inspiration

By far, religion has been the most important source of artistic inspiration. For countless generations Indian artists and craftspeople created works that reflected their religious beliefs. Hinduism, Buddhism, Islam, and other faiths have all had a great influence on the art of India.

When seen for the first time, Hindu art can seem both fantastic and frightening. There are creatures with many heads and Hindu deities with several arms. Many colorful paintings and sculptures show the legendary escapades of the Hindu gods. These stories come from the ancient poems called the *Mahabharata* and the *Ramayana*.

Holy monuments

India is a land of thousands of temples and other holy monuments. A Hindu temple is more than a place of worship. It is a beautiful monument fit for the gods. Inside, the temple looks like a cave with many columns and passageways leading to the temple god at the very center. Rows upon rows of carved stone images decorate the outside of the

temple, which is shaped like a mountain with a peak at the top. Sometimes it is difficult to tell where the building ends and the sculpture begins. In the south the carvings are painted in bright colors; elsewhere the stone is left unpainted. When a section of an old temple wall begins to crumble, craftspeople skilled in the ancient ways create an exact replica with which to replace it.

Cave art

Not all Indian temples are towering buildings. In the eighth century an enormous temple was dug out of pure rock. This cave temple, which is dedicated to Shiva, is located on Elephanta Island in Bombay Harbor. The project must have taken much planning and many years to complete. Carved onto the inside walls of the cave are images of the Hindu god Shiva performing amazing feats.

A touch of Islam

When the Muslim invaders came to India, they brought with them the Islamic style of art. Muslims built mosques with many tall, pointed archways. Instead of creating images and pictures, Islamic artists create intricate designs and beautiful patterns. According to the Muslim faith, it is an insult to Allah to portray anything that was first made by him.

The Taj Mahal is a world-famous labor of love. In the seventeenth century Shah Jahan had the Taj Mahal built in memory of his beloved wife. This monument is also a perfect example of the use of symmetry in art.

Perfect symmetry

Islamic architecture is famous for its use of symmetry. When a design is balanced on each side of a line, symmetry has been achieved. For example, there are always the same number of pillars on either side of the main entry way of many Indian palaces.

The chosen one's palace

One of the finest examples of Islamic architecture is a monument called the Taj Mahal. Made of white marble, the domes, towers, and pools create a scene of perfect symmetry. The marble is encrusted with jewels and precious stones. The Taj Mahal was built to honor the memory of Shah Jahan's wife, Mumtaz Mahal. Her name means "the chosen one of the palace." When she died in 1631, the Shah employed twenty thousand workers to build a tomb for her. The monument took twenty-two years to complete.

At the center of the Taj Mahal is the tomb of the Shah's beloved wife. The tomb is on a square platform behind a carved marble screen. Diamonds, sapphires, and other precious gems are inlaid on the walls. When the emperor died, he was placed in the tomb alongside his wife.

Miniature magnificence

Another art form that was introduced by the Muslim rulers is the technique of miniature painting. Persian artists taught Indian artists their highly colored and detailed style. At one time, miniature paintings were extremely popular among the upper classes and were displayed in palaces and important buildings. The small, realistic paintings depicted court life, Persian stories, and scenes from the Hindu epics.

(top) This ancient Indian painting is actually very small. The art of miniature painting demands great skill and patience, but the lively and colorful result is well worth the effort.

(bottom) While Muslim art tends to be realistic, Hindu temples display fantastic scenes of legendary figures. The many arms of this statue symbolize power.

Everyday crafts

For generations people all over India have expressed themselves creatively by decorating their homes and belongings. Indian creativity has produced everyday objects of extraordinary beauty. A hooked rug, a carved wooden table, brass candlesticks, and handsome jewelry are all examples of common, yet beautiful things.

The art of village artisans

In the past, village craftspeople always made objects that were useful. Today local artisans continue this tradition, fashioning articles that are in demand all over the world. Village crafts include basket-weaving, woodwork, metalwork, pottery, embroidery, and rug-making. To make a basket, a weaver may use bamboo, cane, grasses, reeds, or even fibers from dates or coconuts. Sometimes the weaver makes toys for children, too.

Woven beauty

India has long been famous for the luxurious textiles produced by its skilled village weavers. In fact, India was making textiles two thousand years before anyone in western countries knew how to do it. For many centuries seafarers and traders amazed people back home with fabulous fabrics brought back from India. Indian cloth is still much admired today. Muslin, a light cotton fabric, is so delicate that it has been given the name *nebula venti*, which means "woven winds." The beauty of Indian silk is often enhanced with gold and silver threads. Other textile traditions that come from India are chintz and tie-dye patterned clothes. Different regions are famous for their particular styles. In Rajasthan, for example, small mirrors are embroidered onto skirts. The skills and patterns for making all these different styles are passed down through the generations.

Home decorating

For festivals and special events houses are often decorated inside and out. Pictures of people, flowers, animals, and religious symbols are painted on the walls and around doorways. Rice-flour designs are sometimes made on the floors. Many areas are well known for their unique styles of home decorating.

A rainbow of colors

India is a very colorful country. Indian fabrics and clothes display every shade of the rainbow. Houses come in pastel pinks, blues, and yellows. Multicolored temple sculptures are painted in great detail. Each market and bazaar is a kaleidoscope of the luscious colors of fruits, flowers, and powdered dyes. The whole country is like a giant canvas splashed with happy colors.

A woman displays her latest creations. Many Indians excel in producing beautiful crafts at home in their spare time.

(left) Jewelry-making is an ancient skill carried out by professional craftspeople in large villages. This woman adorns herself with all her worldly treasures as a sign of her wealth and prestige.

(below) The white-washed mud-relief designs on the walls of this desert home are characteristic of houses in the region of Rajasthan. They are always produced by the women of the house.

It is a sunny day, and Nimi and Sarita are laundering clothes. They have just washed a brightly colored *sari*, and each one holds an end of the nine-meter length of cloth. They let it flutter in the wind like a long flag. Worn loosely, the *sari* is typical of most Indian clothing because it is colorful, comfortable, and cool.

The magnificent *sari*

The *sari* is the garment commonly worn by women all over India. It has three parts: a tight blouse, an ankle-length petticoat, and a long cloth between five and nine meters in length that is wrapped around the waist and draped over the shoulder. Many women wear plain *saris* when they work in the fields. Other *saris* are made out of such delicate material that the fabric is almost transparent. The finest ones glitter with threads of gold and silver.

The fishermen below wear cotton **dhotis.**

Buying a new *sari* is a special experience. The buyer sits on a chair in front of a raised platform where the merchant unrolls several bolts of material for her to examine. So many meters of beautifully patterned cottons, silks, and polyester cascade around her that it is often hard to decide which *sari* to buy.

Men's clothing

In northern and central India, village men often wear *dhotis*. A *dhoti* is a piece of white cotton measuring five meters. It is simply wrapped around the waist with either one or both ends drawn up between the legs and tucked into the waistband. There are no buttons, snaps, or zippers. Men sometimes wear long white shirts on top. Loose trousers called pajamas are also popular. The English word pajama comes from two Hindi words: *pa*, which means "leg," and *jama*, which means "garment." The brightly checked or flowered *lungi* is a long, wraparound skirt worn by men in the south. Many men also wear turbans. To make a turban, a long piece of cloth is wound around the head. Turbans come in a variety of bright and pastel colors.

In cities it is common to see men in shirts and trousers. Instead of a western-style business suit, however, many Indian men choose to wear the classical Indian suit, characterized by a long, tight-fitting jacket with a high collar.

Women all over India wear the colorful **sari.**

Punjabi suits

The Punjabi suit is the costume of Sikh women, but many other women in India wear it, as well. The suit has three parts: long pants that narrow at the ankles, a knee-length dress, and a light, flowing scarf. Punjabi suits come in both plain and patterned cottons, silks, and polyesters.

Children's clothes

It is common for small children to wear western-style clothing until they are teenagers. Boys and girls both dress in shorts and shirts, but girls also wear short dresses or blouses and skirts. Children who attend private schools wear uniforms. On special occasions young people put on traditional Indian clothing.

Clothing customs

Clothes often reflect religious traditions. For instance, many Muslim women wear garments that cover their heads and sometimes their faces. Sikh men always wear turbans, and Hindu widows dress in white, the color of mourning.

Although styles of clothing vary from region to region, most Indian clothing is made of cotton. This light and natural textile is ideal for hot weather because it allows the body to breathe. The majority of Indians wear sandals because they are the most practical footwear for a country with a hot and rainy climate.

The sari *is an all-purpose garment that is both comfortable and elegant.*

How to wrap a *sari*

Learning to put on a *sari* properly takes practice. First a woman wraps the cloth around her waist to form a skirt. Then she folds the loose material seven times like a fan. Each fold is about as wide as a hand. The tops of the folds are tucked into her waistband. A woman must check that the hem at the bottom is even. The leftover material is then wrapped around her body and brought up over her left shoulder. The long end of the *sari* drapes gracefully down her back. Sometimes women pull these ends over their heads to form hoods.

Festivals and celebrations

Hardly a day goes by without a festival in India. In fact, there are about thirty major celebrations and numerous local ones throughout the year. Exciting events are held to rejoice in the change of seasons, honor the heroics of legendary figures, and remember national and religious anniversaries. During many religious festivals huge wooden carts carrying statues or shrines are paraded through the streets. Crowds follow along, shouting, chanting, and playing musical instruments.

Celebrating India

India has two holidays to celebrate its nationhood. Independence Day is held on August 15, the anniversary of the day in 1947 when India became an independent country. On this holiday the prime minister makes a speech from the Red Fort in New Delhi.

The most exciting national holiday is Republic Day. On January 26, 1950 the Republic of India was formed. Every year on the anniversary of this day parades are held all over India. The largest parade is held in the capital city of New Delhi, where people from every part of the country join in the huge procession. Decorated elephants and camels march majestically down the street, while airplanes and helicopters provide an awesome airshow. Regional folk dancers perform on a huge stage in the center of the city.

Holi smokes!

Holi, the spring festival, begins with a blazing farewell to the passing season. People say good-bye to the old year with huge bonfires. They rejoice with songs, dances, and plays. The fires symbolize the destruction of the evil spirit Holika.

The most boisterous part of *Holi* occurs on the second day. It is called Color Day because everything and everyone gets splashed with colors. Relatives, friends, and even complete strangers throw colored powders and squirt bright liquids at one another. Nobody goes outside with their good clothes on because they would soon be covered with pink, blue, orange, and yellow blotches. The colors are meant to frighten away evil spirits.

(opposite, left) **When this fellow left home in the morning he was dressed in white! Getting sprayed with brightly colored dyes is what makes** Holi **so much fun.**

(above) **In India people celebrate many colorful festivals such as this Independence Day parade in New Delhi. Everyone wears regional costumes for this huge event.**

Rama's triumph

The festival of *Dussehra* begins with the first new moon of October and lasts for ten nights. It is also known as *Ram Lila* and *Durga Puja*. Every night a different part of a long poem called the *Ramayana* is performed on stages built by the people of every village, town, and city in India. By the end of the festival, the audiences have heard all 48,000 lines of the *Ramayana*.

In each town a narrator recites the story while masked actors in fancy costumes act out the plot. The hero is Prince Rama, who is really the god Vishnu. On the tenth night he rescues his wife Sita from a demon called Ravana. To celebrate Rama's triumph, an enormous model of the demon Ravana is stuffed with straw and firecrackers. An actor dressed as Prince Rama shoots burning arrows at the dummy. Everyone cheers when Ravana explodes, bursting into flame. The crowd then takes part in a lively procession, and people dance in the streets.

A festival of lights

Diwali, which occurs shortly after *Dusshera*, is the Indian New Year. It lasts for five days and marks the end of the monsoon season. The excitement builds as everyone cleans and whitewashes their homes. The whole house, including the doorway, is painted with colorful pictures and designs. In the south of India young women create rice-flour designs on their doorsteps. Family members try to pay off their debts by the fifth day so they can start the new year without owing any money.

Diwali is a time to put on new clothes, eat sweets, visit relatives, exchange gifts, and make offerings to the deities. The highlight of the celebration is the Festival of Lights. Fireworks light up the night sky, and small clay lamps called *dipas* twinkle from every rooftop and windowsill like thousands of stars. These tiny oil lamps are lit to welcome the goddess of wealth, Lakshmi. Merchants worship Lakshmi because they believe she brings prosperity. They compete for her favor by trying to set off the loudest and longest set of firecrackers.

Pongal, festival of the cow

Pongal, an ancient Hindu festival held every January in southern India, marks the end of winter. This three-day event has special customs for each day. On the first day people clean their homes and prepare a sweet called *pongal. Pongal* can be made by boiling a mixture of rice, milk, and brown sugar. This special treat is first offered to the sun and then shared by all. On the second day everyone pays special attention to their cows and bullocks. These beloved animals are decorated with flowers and paint and fed some *pongal.* In the evening everyone goes to see the procession of the decorated cows. Bullfights are held on the third day. In India the bulls are never killed. Instead, small bundles of money are carefully tied to their horns. The contestants try to wrestle the money from the angry bulls without getting hurt. This can be a very dangerous game.

Sikh festivals

Sikh festivals and fairs are staged to celebrate important events in Sikh history and the lives of the *gurus.* The Sikhs also celebrate the Hindu festivals of *Diwali* and *Holi.* They have special reasons for holding these festivals and their own ways of celebrating them. During *Diwali* Sikhs, just like Hindus, light lamps and exchange gifts. The focus of their celebration, however, is remembering the time when an important Sikh leader, Guru Hargobind, was released from captivity. During *Diwali,* the Golden Temple is illuminated in his honor.

*On **Raksha Bandhan** a girl puts a dot of red or yellow powder on her brother's forehead.*

Hola Mohalla

Hola Mohalla is a Sikh festival that takes place the day after the colorful *Holi* festival. It is a three-day fair. Everybody enjoys taking part in the popular horseback riding and athletic competitions. Drawing on stories from the past, Sikh men stage mock battles using traditional weapons. Afterwards everyone dances, sings, and feasts.

Id-ul Fitr

Id-ul Fitr is the Muslim festival held to mark the end of the fast of *Ramadan.* Every year it begins one week earlier than it did the year before. For the month of *Ramadan,* Muslims do not eat anything between sunrise and sunset. They do this to recall the time when the prophet Muhammad fasted while awaiting Allah's message. At the end of the month-long fast, families prepare feasts, and everyone gathers at the mosques to pray. After leaving the mosques they rejoice and, bearing gifts of food, they visit friends.

Raksha Bandhan

Raksha Bandhan is a special celebration for brothers and sisters. In July sisters buy or make bracelets called *rakhi* to give to their brothers. The bracelets can be made of colored ribbon or thread. The custom of giving bracelets comes from an ancient legend about the god Indra. Before battle Indra's wife tied a *rakhi* around his wrist to protect him. Now sisters do the same for their brothers to show their affection.

Seven wedding promises

A Hindu wedding is both a joyous and a sad occasion. People are happy because two families are joining together and a couple is beginning a new life. At the same time they are sad because, after the ceremony, the bride must leave her parents to become part of her husband's family. Sometimes the bride and groom barely know each other because the marriage has been arranged by the two families. Let's join Sanjeev and Neelam, a young couple, in the preparations for their important day.

Customs to bring good luck

Many good-luck customs are part of the preparations. It is customary for the bride and groom not to see each other for a whole month before the wedding. Another custom is called the *mehndi* ritual. On the night before the ceremony the bride's sisters get together to paint lacy designs on the palms of Neelam's hands and the soles of her feet. They use a natural paint made from the leaves of the henna plant. At first the dye is green, but when Neelam washes her hands and feet the next morning, the designs magically become bright red, which is considered a lucky color. The houses are also decorated, and a special canopy is built for the bride and groom.

Marriage symbols

Along with a magnificent red silk *sari*, Neelam wears many shining glass bangles and all the gold jewelry her family can provide. Sanjeev gives her a necklace of black beads called a *mangal sutra* or "blessed thread." The *mangal sutra* is a symbol of marriage. As long as Sanjeev lives, Neelam will never take it off. The jeweled medallion that hangs in the center of Neelam's forehead, the red powder in the part of her hair, and the red dot on her forehead are all signs of a married woman.

Welcome to the family!

On the morning of the wedding Neelam's oldest brother, Shiv, goes to the house of Sanjeev's family with gifts. These gifts seal the union of the two families. When the gifts are accepted, Shiv puts a bit of sandalwood paste on Sanjeev's forehead. Dressed in elaborate clothing, a headdress, and garlands of flowers, Sanjeev drives to Neelam's house in a white car. A young boy accompanies him to bring good luck. Some Indian grooms ride white horses to their weddings. A few even arrive on white elephants.

(opposite) Neelam and Sanjeev pose for a wedding picture after the ceremony. Traditional Hindu weddings are full of ancient customs and symbols. For instance, Neelam wears a red **sari***, and the couple is draped with customary golden tassles and flower garlands.*

Sanjeev arrived at the wedding in this extravagantly decorated white wedding car. A wandering cow cannot resist the fresh flowers and plants.

The ceremony

Neelam's family welcomes Sanjeev with a garland of flowers. During the ceremony the couple sits around a sacred fire under a canopy. Agni, the god of fire, is part of the ceremony because he is considered to be the most truthful god. A Brahmin priest performs the ceremony by chanting special wedding prayers. Sanjeev's white scarf is tied to the end of Neelam's *sari*. Knotted together, the bride and groom walk around the fire seven times as Sanjeev makes seven promises. He promises to keep Neelam happy, share his feelings and possessions with her, to be faithful, respect her family, and to make her a part of his life. The seventh promise is to keep the other six promises! After the ceremony, the celebrations begin.

 # Performing arts

Music, dance, and drama are called performing arts because the artists actually perform in front of audiences. Indians believe that both music and dance are gifts from the gods. Many plays tell dramatic stories taken from Hindu folklore.

Magical music

The classical music of India has a magical sound. Its three basic parts are the *raga*, the *tala*, and the *drone*. The *raga* is a series of little melodies played over and over. Each one represents an emotion, a season, or a time of day. In all there are seventy thousand *ragas*! The *tala* is the rhythm of the music, which is either clapped or played on drums. India can be called the land of drums because there are so many different types used in Indian music.

(above) This gesture means anger. Indian dancers use movements and facial expressions that are thousands of years old.

The *drone* is a constant tone that is usually played by a single instrument. In combination, the *raga*, *tala*, and *drone* create the desired mood for a musical piece.

(below) These musicians play ancient tunes and rhythms.

North and south

The *sitar*, *tabla*, and the *sarangi* are classical northern Indian musical instruments that are well known around the world. Most *sitars* have six or seven main strings and up to nineteen "sympathetic" strings. Instead of being plucked, sympathetic strings vibrate when the main strings are played. The *sitar* is made from a large hollow gourd, and its long arm is teak wood. The *tabla* is a pair of drums resembling bongo drums. The *sarangi* is a stringed instrument played with a bow. It is carved out of a single block of wood, has three or four main strings, and as many as forty sympathetic strings. The music of the *sarangi* reminds many people of the human voice. A *shehnai*, a wind instrument that resembles a small clarinet, produces the constant *drone* sound.

The music of the south differs somewhat from that of the north. For example, the stringed *vina* is used in place of the *sitar*. The *drone* is provided by a *tempura*, another type of stringed instrument. The flutelike *veenu* and the *mrdangam* drum are also southern instruments.

Divine dancing

According to Hindu belief dancing came from the gods. The laws of art, music, and dance are recorded in an ancient text that is part of the sacred Hindu scriptures called the *Natya Sastra*. This book of rules was written by Bharata Muni, who is believed to have been taught to dance by the god Shiva. Shiva is called the "lord of the dance." Many of the poses used by Indian dancers today look just like the poses carved on ancient temple walls.

Indian dance styles vary from region to region. Some tell stories; others entertain audiences with beautiful movements. Many Indian dancers wear bells on their ankles, lots of gold and silver jewelry, and colorful, flowing costumes. Rather than move around a lot, they dance from a bended-knee position and stamp their feet to complicated rhythms. Dancers delight their audiences with hundreds of symbolic hand gestures and many dramatic facial expressions. They are able to move their necks, eyeballs, and eyebrows in the most fascinating ways.

Bharata Natyam

In southern India *Bharata Natyam* is the favorite dance form. In the past this dance was performed in Hindu temples. The movements of the dancers represent human emotions. Flowing costumes and striking makeup add to the effect of the dance. The dancers wear flowers in their long, braided hair. Their fingers are dipped in henna dye, and their feet have slippers painted on them.

The combined effect of a dancer's makeup, costume, and graceful skill is simply mesmerizing.

This traveling troupe is staging a Hindu legend. What role is the boy in blue playing?

Dramatic dances

India has a rich tradition of dance and folk dramas. Troupes of performers travel from village to village where they tell religious tales through action and dance. Most of these tales come from the famous poems, the *Mahabharata* and *Ramayana*, which contain legends of the deities.

Manipuri

In eastern India performers dance in the soft and gentle *manipuri* style. The *manipuri* dancers tell the legend of *Ras Lila*. Long ago Krishna, the Hindu god of love, met a group of cowherd maidens. Under the moonlit sky, Krishna played soft melodies on his flute. The music was so beautiful that it cast a spell on the maidens. Krishna led them into a circle so he could dance with them. He danced so fast that he seemed to be everywhere at once, and each maiden thought he was dancing with her alone.

Today *manipuri* dancers retell this story. Krishna is played by a male dancer. Girls or young women wear colorful bell-shaped skirts made

of material that has little pieces of glass or mirror sewn into it. The glass sparkles as the dancers twirl. The dancers pile their hair up high and drape transparent veils over their heads and faces. The young women dance around the male dancer in a circle—first slowly and then quickly. Gracefully they sway and turn, keeping time with painted wands.

Kathakali

The *kathakali* dance drama has been staged in the state of Kerala since the seventeenth century. *Kathakali* plays are based on stories found in the *Mahabharata*. In fact, *kathakali* means "story play." While vocalists recite the legend, performers dramatize it with exaggerated body, face, and eye movements. The plays are often performed outside. Full-length plays begin at nightfall and last until sunrise. Drums announce the beginning of the play. Dancers enchant their audiences with their forceful steps and the sound of a hundred jingling ankle bells.

Great get-ups

Costumes are tremendously elaborate, and dancers always wear symbolic makeup. The hero has a green face and wears a crown that looks like an upside-down vase. He also wears a *chutti*, a white ridged beard made from rice paste. It is molded right onto his face. The demon wears red makeup, a red beard, and an elaborate halo. He may also have a wart on his forehead or nose. The bigger the wart, the more wicked the character. Female characters, played by young boys, are yellow. Thieves wear black, and priests have long white beards. Makeup artists mix colored powders with oil and apply the paint with a long piece of bamboo. It can take up to four hours to complete a makeup job.

The costumes, movements, and stories of kathakali are the same in every performance. All the parts are played by men.

Tough training

Kathakali is traditionally performed by men. In the past *kathakali* training was used as a type of military training for young boys because it was so demanding. A young boy begins his apprenticeship at the age of ten. For eight or ten years he follows a rigid exercise schedule in order to develop the necessary muscle control required for the fancy footwork and hand gestures. The postures are very difficult. With feet spread apart, bent knees, and arched backs, dancers must learn to balance their weight on the outsides of their feet.

The flavors of India

Walk into any Indian restaurant in the world and you will smell delicious spices. The wonderful aromas of saffron, cumin, cinnamon, nutmeg, and ginger linger in nearly every Indian household. For festivals and celebrations cooks spend extra time and effort preparing family favorites. To the Indian, food is worthy of being offered to the gods. Before serving a meal, a sample of the food is often placed as an offering in the family's household shrine.

The spice of life

Spices are used in every Indian dish, but only some of them make food taste hot. Indians like to flavor their foods with everything from the delicate flavor of fresh coriander leaves to the red-hot bite of chili peppers. India has a perfect climate for growing all kinds of spices, and many are exported all over the world. Caraway, cardamom, chili peppers, cinnamon, cloves, coriander, and cumin are just the spices that begin with the letter "c."

Curried *kari?*

An item that you may find on your kitchen spice rack is a bottle labelled "curry powder." Curry is not one spice but several spices ground up and mixed together. An Indian cook would never use a premixed curry powder when preparing dinner. She or he picks out a unique blend of spices for every dish and then grinds them up into a fine powder using a mortar and pestle. Freshly ground spices are more flavorful than preground ones.

People all over the world mistakenly believe that Indian food consists merely of dishes flavored with curry. In fact, there is no single dish called curry in India. The word curry comes from the Tamil word *kari*, which simply means "a stewlike dish." There are numerous *karis*, and Indians know each one by its unique flavor and name.

Foods of southern India

Most people in the south are Hindu and are, therefore, strict vegetarians. If they are lucky enough to live along the coastline, they likely eat seafood dishes. Most people eat rice at every meal. About a thousand varieties of rice can be found in India. The lovely fragrance and flavor of the most popular rice, basmati, whets many appetites. Rice is often eaten in combination with a *kari* or *dhal*. *Dhal* is a thick souplike dish made from lentils. Sometimes it can be quite spicy. In southern India *dhal* is a thin liquid, whereas *dhal* in the north resembles a thick pea soup.

Favorite fruits

Tropical fruit markets in the south overflow with every color of the rainbow: pink melons, green mangos, red pomegranates, orange papayas, yellow bananas, lemons, and jackfruit. A jackfruit, which is really a vegetable, has a prickly outer skin and yellow meat inside. Coconut trees grow well in tropical climates. People drink the milk or add it to sauces and chutneys.

Foods of northern India

Indian cooking in the north has been influenced by the large Muslim population. More people eat meat in northern India than in the south, but never pork. A special type of outdoor oven is used to bake *tandoori* dishes. Before cooking, goat meat, fish, or chicken is soaked overnight in a mixture of yogurt and spices. This process, called marinating, adds a distinctive flavor. Then the meat is grilled in an outdoor, cone-shaped clay oven called a *tandoori* oven.

Instead of having rice at every meal, northern Indians eat a variety of breads. Indian breads are flat and round. *Chapati* is shaped like a pancake and made with a special flour. *Paratha*, a crispy, fried bread, is sometimes stuffed with vegetables. *Nan* is puffy and oval shaped. A very common meal in the north is *dhal*, vegetables, and *chapati* bread.

How to make *chapatis*

You need:

>   230 mL (1 1/3 cups) *chapati* flour or
>   whole wheat flour
>   185 mL (3/4 cup) water
>   rolling pin, cookie sheet, bowl

Pour flour into a bowl. Slowly add water, mixing it in with your fingers. Pick up dough and knead it for ten minutes until it is smooth and elastic. Place in a bowl, cover with a cloth, and leave for an hour.

Knead the dough again. Sprinkle flour on a rolling pin and onto a large, clean surface. Pull off a piece of dough about the size of a ping-pong ball and roll it out. Sprinkle on lots of flour to keep the *chapati* from sticking to the rolling pin and table. The *chapati* should be very thin and without wrinkles. Place *chapatis* on a cookie sheet.

With adult supervision, preheat the oven to 150°C (300°F). Cook the *chapatis* for about ten minutes or until they turn light brown. Keep watching. You don't want them to burn! Put your *chapatis* aside in a towel-lined basket to keep them warm, and serve them with stew, soup, or a *kari*.

Mealtime manners

Most Indians do not eat with knives or forks and, in some areas, people eat their meals on banana leaves instead of dishes. Diners wash their hands both before and after the meal. Instead of using utensils, Indians eat with their right hand. They never use the left hand—it is considered bad manners! In the south people only eat with their fingertips, but in the north people sometimes scoop up the food with their whole hand. Small pieces of bread are broken off and used for scooping.

Desserts

Indians love to eat sweet foods. At special times they even offer them to their deities. At the end of a meal the usual dessert is fruit. On special occasions, however, there is an endless variety of desserts from which to choose. Many of the desserts are made by boiling milk with sugar and cardamom pods until only a thick syrup is left. Different fruits or vegetables are then added to this liquid. The resulting desserts have a fudgelike quality. The recipe for Indian ice cream, below, has been simplified to eliminate the boiling milk. This simpler version can be made safely and easily. The result is almost the same.

Indian ice cream

You need:

>   1 can, 300 mL (1 1/4 cups) condensed milk
>   1 small can, 160 mL (3/4 cup) evaporated milk
>   250 mL (1 cup) whipping cream
>   125 mL (1/2 cup) almonds
>   125 mL (1/2 cup) mango, blueberries,
>   kiwi fruit, strawberries, peaches,
>   bananas, or other fruits of your choice.

Put all the ingredients into a blender and blend well. If you are using blueberries, you may want to stir them in at the end. Pour mixture into a shallow plastic dish with a lid. Freeze until ice cream is solid. Cut into slices and serve. You can also pour the mixture into ice-cube trays if you prefer to eat them like popsicles. Cover the trays with plastic wrap and insert popsicle sticks by poking holes through the wrap when the ice cream has begun to harden.

Along with a wide range of traditional cultural activities, India also offers modern entertainment. People attend rock concerts, watch television, travel on tours across the country, and go to action-packed films.

Going to the movies

Indians love going to the movies. Each week seventy million Indians watch their favorite stars perform. Sometimes they wait for several hours in long line-ups. In villages where there are no movie theaters, make-shift theaters are constructed. Sheets are hung up outside for use as movie screens. Indian movies are usually musicals that tell stories of love and adventure. Much of India's popular music comes from these films. Recently, more and more documentary films are being produced each year. These are serious films that cover India's social issues. Over eight hundred feature productions are made in India every year.

Street performers

While walking on a city street or through a busy bazaar, a person is likely to come across several street performers. These multi-talented entertainers put on shows wherever they can find an audience—often in the center of a crowded market. There are acrobats, magicians, jugglers, puppeteers, and snake charmers. Everyone gathers around to see the act. No one has to pay, but some leave a few coins if they like the show. Circuses are also popular. Circus troupes tour the country, setting up their tents on the outskirts of villages and cities.

Games and sports

Almost every kind of sport and game imaginable is popular in India. Field hockey, soccer, cricket, polo, badminton, and volleyball are just a few of the sports played both nationally and internationally. Indians have also invented games, many of which are now enjoyed all over the world.

The origins of chess

Chess is an Indian game developed in ancient times. It used to be called *chaturanga*, which refers to the four divisions of the army: elephants, horses, chariots, and foot soldiers. Today these divisions are represented by pawns, knights, bishops, and rooks. At one time Indian princes played the game using live people instead of chess pieces. One difference between Indian chess and international chess is that there is no queen in Indian chess. A playing piece called a *vizier* is used instead.

Bowled for a duck

An extremely popular sport in India, cricket is played between two teams of eleven players. The teams play in fields or large open areas. Although the pitcher is called a bowler, cricket is not at all like bowling. In fact, to be "bowled for a duck" in a game of cricket is almost like striking out in baseball.

A small, hard ball, a paddle-shaped bat, and two wickets are needed to play the game. A wicket is made up of three waist-high stakes called stumps pushed into the ground. Small sticks called bails are laid across the top of the stakes. The batter stands in front of the wicket. The bowler from the other team throws the ball, attempting to hit the wicket to get the batter out. When the wicket is hit, the bails fall off, indicating that the batter is out. The batter tries to hit the ball to keep it away from the wicket and send it out into the field. When the ball is hit, the batter and another of his or her teammates run back and forth between the two wickets to score runs. They keep earning runs until the other team returns the ball and hits a wicket. When ten batters are out, the other team has a turn up at bat.

(opposite, top) The most popular team sport in India is cricket. These players meet every Sunday for a game.

(opposite, right) Many Indians who live near the ocean visit the beach on sunny afternoons.

Hold your breath and run!

Kabaddi is a village team sport for people with good lungs. One player runs into the opponent's territory and tags one or more members from the other team. The player then tries to make it back home without being stopped by the players he or she just tagged. All this is done in a single breath. To prove that the player has not taken a breath, he or she constantly calls out *"kabbaddi-kabbaddi-kabbaddi."* If the runner succeeds in making it home, all the opponent's players that were tagged are out.

Many ways to enjoy

Whether you attend a colorful festival, indulge in a vegetarian feast, or take a quiet walk on one of India's many beaches, you cannot help but appreciate the beauty of this land and the richness of India's culture.

Glossary

art form - A type of creation that is especially beautiful or meaningful

artisan - A skilled craftsperson

Buddhism - A religion founded by Buddha, an ancient religious leader from India

caste system - An ancient Indian social system that classifies people according to birth

chintz - A many-colored cotton fabric

Christianity - A religion based on the belief that Jesus Christ is the son of God

civilization - A society with a well-established culture that has existed for a long period of time

cremate - To burn a body to ashes

culture - The customs, beliefs, and arts of a distinct group of people

curry - A mixture of ground-up spices; a stewlike dish

deity - A god or goddess

embroidery - Intricate designs sewn with a needle and thread

epic - A long poem about the adventures of legendary heroes or deities

generation - People born at about the same time. Grandparents, parents, and children make up three generations.

heritage - The customs, achievements, and history passed on from earlier generations; tradition

Hinduism - An ancient Indian religion based on the holy books called the *Vedas*

Islam - A religion founded by the prophet Muhammad. Its followers are called Muslims.

Jainism - An Indian religion based on the teachings of Mahavira

marinate - To soak in a flavorful liquid before cooking

meditation - The act of emptying the mind of all thought in order to achieve a state of inner peace

mosque - A sacred building in which Muslims worship

procession - A group of people walking together as part of a ceremony. Processions are common in Indian festivals.

prophet - A religious leader believed to be inspired by God or a spirit

reincarnation - The endless cycle of birth, death, and rebirth of the same soul

ritual - A formal custom in which several steps are faithfully followed

sandalwood - A type of tree valued for its fragrant oil and yellow paste product

shrine - A structure that is dedicated to a deity

Sikhism - An Indian religion based on the teachings of Guru Nanak

symbol - Something that represents or stands for something else

tolerance - A willingness to be patient towards people whose opinions and actions differ from one's own

vegetarian - A person who does not eat meat

western - The term used to describe people from the western part of the world, especially Europe and North America, as opposed to people from Asia, such as Indians and Chinese

whitewash - To paint a thin, white liquid on walls and other surfaces

Index

9 WP Printed in U.S.A. 9 8 7